PCs

for Peewees

Helping pre-schoolers get the best out of computers

Nicole Taylor

PCs for Peewees

Helping pre-schoolers get the best out of computers

Nicole Taylor

© Nicole Taylor 2008

Published by 1stWorld Publishing
P. O. Box 2211, Fairfield, Iowa 52556
tel: 641-209-5000 • fax: 866-440-5234
web: www.1stworldpublishing.com

LCCN: 2008908476

SoftCover ISBN: 978-1-4218-9030-2

eBook ISBN: 978-1-4218-9031-9

This material has been written and published solely for educational purposes. The author and the publisher shall have neither liability or responsibility to any person or entity with respect to any loss, damage or injury caused or alleged to be caused directly or indirectly by the information contained in this book.

With thanks to senteacher.org
Learning and teaching Scotland

And special thanks to my son Mark
for being such an inspiration

Contents

Introduction

We live in an age where young children have many opportunities to see computers being used in a variety of contexts.

Computers are used more generally in the home, seen on television, found in schools and are becoming more common in nurseries. It is just as normal for children to have computers around them, as having a tricycle or Lego™ bricks so why shouldn't youngsters have fun using a PC or a laptop?

It is a fact that with their receptive minds and natural capacity for learning, children can absorb new skills quickly, for example, social and language skills. This extends to skills in using equipment.

I have been teaching computer use to adults for many years and have always had a PC in my home. However, the last thing I intended was to let my toddler loose on such an expensive and delicate piece of equipment.

But when I noticed the interest my younger son showed in what I was doing on the computer, I was impressed enough to let him try using it. The outcome was fascinating.

He was like a sponge soaking up all the skills I was showing him. He watched, asked me how then completed what he wanted to do. Within a week his mouse skills were better than a lot of my 'adult' students

He learnt to spell his name and to understand that 'www' was for the Internet; his hand-eye co-ordination improved with each session—all this at barely two years old!

Although when my son started using the computer he was on my actual work PC,

I was lucky enough to have a second PC in my house available for him. I obtained this older computer second hand from an office that was updating its system; although old it was adequate for the kids.

I didn't set the second computer up straight away for him to use as I thought that the novelty of playing with mine would soon wear off. When it became apparent that his interest continued unabated (and I realised the benefit of a computer to his learning), I set 'his' PC up next to mine.

There is a wealth of games and learning aids available in shops and on the Internet for preschoolers to encourage independent learning through working with numbers, letters, animals, shapes and colours.

When young children learn a second language it gives them a considerable advantage in learning another. The same concept applies to learning to use computers where the skills children acquire help them to adapt easily to using and understanding other forms of technology. As we older kids know, technology is a field that changes very quickly.

By helping your child to use the computer you are not only teaching them PC skills but also reinforcing the skill of learning: learning to achieve, to enjoy learning and to respect complex equipment. As children grow they will favour some activities over others but the learning skill itself is transferable.

I have seen in my teaching career many times, that those people who have barriers to learning find that when they connect enjoyably with the process of taking in new information they want to learn more: whether it's computer skills, English language or learning to play the guitar.

Once young children experience fun with learning, it makes future learning experiences easier. You are your child's first teacher; make it count.

Getting Started

Your files

Protecting your own work

Before you let your little one loose on your computer it would be a good idea to make sure your own work is protected. It's amazing what they manage to navigate through and add their own little touches to, such as zzzzzzzzzzzzzzz or ddjidjdii or pressing the magic button that makes everything vanish.

You can protect your work in a number of ways;

⤷ Create a copy of all your work

⤷ Password your files

⤷ Setting up a separate user profile

> **Protecting your work now, can save problems later**

Creating a copy of all your work *see page 60*

You should, as a general rule back up your work on a regular basis. It depends on how often you use your computer but either daily, weekly or fortnightly is the norm.

Then if something did get 'redesigned' by your technical tot, you could easily get a copy of your previous work from your back up files.

Passwording your files *see page 61*

Putting a password to your individual files and folders saves anything happening to your work in the first place. However if your files get damaged or lost for some reason, for example, with a virus attack, the only way to get your work back is if you backed up your work previously.

The password option may be suitable for your important documents only as trying to password all of them, depending on how many you have, could take ages.

Setting up a separate user profile *See page 62*

I would say this is the most suitable option for saving and protecting your work while giving your youngster freedom to move around the computer.

You set up a separate logon for your child that has no administrator rights so that, for example they cannot get into the workings of the computer or download extra software from the Internet.

Ergonomics

Whether you are using a PC or a laptop, it is very important to help your child maintain the correct posture when using the computer.

In the UK, more than one million people a year suffer from musculoskeletal disorders[1] which result in backaches, headaches, eye strain, Carpal Tunnel Syndrome (CTS) and Repetitive Strain Injury (RSI), partly due to incorrect posture and lack of regular breaks when using a computer; in the US 33% of working days were lost because of these problems[2].

Ensuring your toddler uses the correct posture right from the start will benefit their learning and long term health.

Back

The toddler's back and neck should be straight, preferably with their back against the back of the chair. If the monitor is too high or too low, it will cause their neck to be at an angle and encourage them to sit slanted.

Hands

Children should be able to use the mouse and keyboard comfortably without having to over-stretch their arms or reduce the flexibility of the arms through lacking adequate space.

The wrist should not 'arch' or 'bend' and the elbows should be at right angles, bending naturally from the shoulders.

Eyes

Leading opticians advise the monitor should be at 60 cm (24 inches) from your child's eyes. You may need to adjust the distance depending on the size of screen.

---

1 British Health and Safety Executive
2 U.S. Department of Labor

Breaks

Even though your toddler may enjoy what they are doing and not want to stop, you need to ensure that they take regular breaks away from the screen and from their chair.

They should move their eyes away from the screen every 5 – 10 minutes for about 15 seconds to refocus and rest the eye muscles.

To redirect their eyes from the screen briefly, the easiest way is to talk to them. Ask them how they are or what they are doing and get them to look at you; or you can show them something such as a particular colour somewhere in the room or on their clothing that matches one they are looking at on the screen. For example, 'Dora® is wearing red shorts; can you see anything red in the room?'

They should take a complete break from the computer every 15 – 20 minutes. You can use some of the activities found on the computer to distract and move them, colouring, dancing or songs found on the Internet.

Chances are that your toddler will want to stop computer activities and do something else after a while anyway.

Hardware and assistive devices

Depending on your toddler's needs, you can buy extra devices to aid little hands, make computers colourful and save your keyboard from accidental spills.

These can all be used in addition to your regular hardware.

Mouse replacements

Big mice

Good for little hands and fingers.

Switches

Switches are good for children who have limited mobility in their arms, fingers or body *see page* 60

Keyboard equipment

Big keys

For easier access to keys

Key guards

To stop your toddler's fingers slipping onto other keys

Keyboard covers

To save your keyboard from accidental spills or dribbles

Extra devices

Graphics tablets

This can be used to help draw objects or letters

Microscope

You can enlarge small objects, such as insects, plants or food

Microphone

So you and your child can record songs together

This is by no means a complete list. You can find more information on suitable websites for these and other hardware *on page 71*.

When buying hardware, make sure it will be compatible with your computer, especially if your computer is more than five years old.

Most extra devices are USB compatible.

Teaching tips

Although your child can pick up computer use quickly, do not push them into using the computer as this is a sure-fire way to put them off.

Teaching and learning should be a wonderful experience for both of you. There are a few simple steps to teaching.

⌐ Encouragement

⌐ Demonstration

⌐ Practice

⌐ Praise

Show them different parts of the computer

You can start by using the computer as you normally do.

1. Try to encourage your child to sit with you while explaining what you are doing. You can also show them the different parts of the PC such as mouse and keyboard.

It helps to talk about any pictures on the screen and the different letters that appear as you type.

This shows your toddler that the computer is interactive and a means of communication.

2. When the time comes for your toddler to start using the computer, let them take control of the mouse or keyboard just to get a feel of the hardware. If the mouse arrow isn't going straight or they are typing lots of letters in random places do not worry, it's all part of the learning process.

When you feel the time is right, you can then introduce your child to a directed activity, guessing games work well. For example, if you had a game loaded, ask: 'What would happen if you press the mouse here (on the relevant section)? Or if you had a DVD in, ask: 'What would happen if you press the play button?' Show the child where to click or press while talking them through what you are doing and what is going to happen.

3. Next comes practise. Let them have a go at selecting information or icons with the mouse. If they are having difficulty using the mouse, try putting your hand on top of theirs to gently guide them.

It may take a little while for them to get the hang of using the mouse and they may at times feel a little frustrated. If this happens, you can either take it in turns to move the mouse or be very subtle about your help.

At the toddler stage when children are discovering their own power and independence they may not like you helping them.

Once you get to the fun part of the games, using the mouse will soon become second nature for your child.

4. When they have managed to move the mouse to the right spot or clicked the correct mouse button give them a big cheer; something I'm sure you're used to doing. In fact you'll be so proud of them you won't be able to help yourself.

Such praise should continue throughout their time on the computer.

Engage their interest

Whether you are teaching letters, numbers, music or how to turn the computer on, to be successful you need to engage your learner's interest.

If they or you are not really that interested to start with, it will be an uphill struggle. There are some simple ways you can engage your child:

🖰 **Voice tone** – try to make what you are going to do exciting or mysterious.

🖰 **Body language** – if you are standing or sitting next to or slightly behind them try to lean inwards towards your child as you would if they were showing you something. This will encourage them to feel that they are in control and trusted with your computer.

🖰 **Pictures** – Images and icons are great for recognition of programs and activities.

Further help is given on teaching tips in the chapters that follow.

Using the Internet

The World Wide Web

Use the web to integrate with every day activities

There is a wealth of learning opportunities for your toddler on the Internet.

They can play and learn with their favourite TV characters, find out about different animals or places and have loads of fun along the way.

Using the computer shouldn't be an activity separated from everyday life but integrated with it.

You can look at trees or ducks on the computer with your toddler before taking a visit to the park. If you go to the zoo, you can create an image diary of all animals that you both saw. Find recipes, places you have both visited and more. Search and do—look for an item then follow it up with an activity or vice versa.

This routine helps your child to view the PC as an extended learning opportunity as well as a source of games and communication.

By using the computer as a tool to help toddlers to participate in activities it can help to keep your children active as well as develop other life and learning skills.

Internet safety

Internet security is an obvious concern for parents of children of all ages. There are a number of options you can choose to keep your toddler's viewing innocent.

- Pop-up blocker
- Firewall
- Child search engines
- Net-nanny programs

These programs are all designed to keep your computers safe from any adult content from appearing on your screen.

For further advice on which product to choose speak with your Internet Service Provider.

Browsing

As you start to teach your child to use the Internet, starting each session by showing them the Internet browser icon on your desktop will help them recognise how to start using the Internet. Once your child is familiar with it you can ask them to point to the icon that starts the Internet, or in their language, the picture that takes them to their game.

> **Many website games have structured learning aims for younger children**

It is a good idea to have the homepage of the browser set to a a show or character that your child likes, so they immediately see something enjoyable once you have logged on to the Internet. You may need to change the picture regularly depending on how quickly they change favourite characters. To change the homepage *See page 63.*

Once you have logged on to the Internet and chosen the website for your child, you can then start playing the games together.

Many of the games themselves have structured learning aims, such as counting or identifying shapes and colours. The underlining goals for many of the games include improving the child's basic skills in literacy and numeracy as well as developing their mouse and motor skills.

Your child's hand-eye co-ordination can improve rapidly but children differ in the pace they develop computer skills, just as they do with walking, talking and growing.

If your child is still interested in the computer after a few weeks, that is progress in itself.

Websites

The best place to start with finding a suitable website can be with your child's favourite character. Popular characters like Dora the Explorer® or Winnie the Pooh® usually have a website that can easily be found in your preferred search engine.

Another source of great children's websites is your regional or national television network; they often have a children's section with links to sites about the TV programmes that particular network airs.

The advantage in using websites is that you are not restricted by the region or country you live in. You have complete access to what is available for children from around the world.

There are some excellent websites you can enjoy with your preschoolers a list of which can be found *on page 69.*

Literacy

Recognising letters

W W W W W W: this is the letter key my son kept pressing every time we sat at the computer. He picked the letter out when we were reading books and when we saw it while watching TV.

At first I thought that he just liked that particular letter until one day when I logged on to the Internet and he pointed to the address bar, said, 'wwwww' and *'Go Diego Go®'* (his favourite program at the time) that I realised that he actually meant the www. to log onto a website.

From watching me log on so many times, he realised that that was what you do to get to a website. He had started to associate letters other than those of his own name, with meaning.

After a few weeks of his playing games with his favourite characters on the Internet, it was evident that he wanted to try something else with letters. He would type his name and press random letters into the search engine box. I decided to go along with this interest in typing and opened my word-processing program for him to use.

I changed the size of the letter font so that he had a better view of what he was typing as well as the colour to make it look more interesting for him and there you have it: not only was he learning about letters but also how to make the text bigger and change its colour.

Letter Games

1. When introducing letters, try starting with something personal to your child such as their name.

To guide children with the letters, point out the letters they need on the keyboard for them to type saying each letter as they type it.

2. As your child progresses, ask them to find other letters; for example, ask: 'Where's the W?'

3. Hold a copy of the letter or point it out from a book and ask them to find it on the keyboard.

Teaching tips

🖐 As you are teaching your child, remember to keep it in the context of something they are interested in or turn it into a game.

🖐 Reinforce what they are spelling: 'That's Mark's name' or 'That says dog, D-O-G'.

🖐 To add further variety to the letters you can change the size, text style and colour. Depending on your child's age, you can do this for them or do it together.

🖐 To support their knowledge of the basic icons, you can ask them to point to the buttons that change the size, text style or colour of letters.

Upper case versus lower case letters

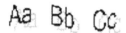

If the keyboard you are using has a standard QWERTY layout, the letters on the keys will be in upper case.

To save confusing young children when they start typing or copying words, it will help if you set the keyboard to type in upper case (put the Caps Lock on) and change the font to 'Arial' so the letters onscreen correspond with the letters on the keyboard.

When children learn the alphabet in school or nursery, they are introduced to lower case letters first. However I have found it easier to teach toddlers and others unfamiliar with the alphabet to recognise the upper case letters and words onscreen first. Doing it this way round does not interfere with a child's recognition of lower case letters later on.

Once your child is confident with knowing the position of the keys on the keyboard, you may want to introduce the lower case letters onscreen. Many alphabet cards that can be bought or are in books, commonly have both upper and lower case letters together so your youngster can gain familiarity with both forms.

You can reinforce the link between upper and lower case letters by asking your toddler if you or they should type a 'big A' or 'little a'.

Developing words

Once your child is comfortable with knowing most of the alphabet, you can move on to looking at words.

Your child may already to be able to spell their own name so you can extend their enthusiasm for spelling to other small words quite easily.

Word recognition is also improved when your youngster looks at a picture of the word you are describing from a book or a website. Below are some simple words your toddler can learn.

Bed	Bee
Chair	Bird
Table	Pizza
Pen	Apple
Cup	Rain
Book	Sun
Tree	Moon

Pictures can be found easily on the Internet, or cut out from magazines or catalogues.

Practising recognition of these words can be continued whenever there is an opportunity: when you are making dinner, driving in the car or going for a walk.

It is not the idea to teach perfect spelling or grammar, but to have fun looking at the scope of typed letters: how one letter can become big or small and two or more letters joined together can make a whole new word and eventually, how new words together can make magical stories.

Word games to play

1. Count the letters

Choose a word and then ask how many of a particular letter there is. For example: 'How many letter Es in Elephant?' This exercise also helps to develop number skills.

2. Missing letters.

Type a word your child knows, for example, their name, with one letter missing and ask them to fill in the gap.

3. What does this start with?

Show a picture of a common object, for example, a tree, and ask your child to find or point to the letter it begins with on the keyboard. For younger children it may help to say the letter they are looking for or it may be too difficult for them to guess.

To develop this game further you could offer a choice of two or three letters on paper; when your child has chosen the right letter, ask them to find it on the keyboard.

Numeracy

Developing number skills

There is huge scope for physical activity and creativity when exploring maths

Numeracy is not just about calculations. Positive numeracy skills enable us to choose the right TV channel, tell the time, make a telephone call and identify shapes, to name a few practical uses.

Try this for yourself: from where you are sitting, take a look around and observe how many things there are with numbers on them or how many objects of different shapes and sizes there are.

Your toddler can explore in a physical and creative way such concepts such as distance, size, shape and quantity.

In later life, the early understanding of numeracy concepts is essential to success in careers such as architecture or design; and in sporting and leisure activities from gymnastics and dance to playing pool.

Playing number games, with discussion and questions, also benefits the toddler's development of language and thought patterns.

The best way of helping your child to develop number skills is to explore with them how numbers are integrated in everyday life. All around them are things of different shapes and sizes, each of which is used for a different purpose.

Think of the shapes you can both create with your hands or using card, or the different objects you can use for counting or measuring. Have fun helping your child to tap into their natural creativity and to develop their imagination: something that toddlers have bucket loads of!

Number games to play

1. Count and type

Count something around the house with your child, such as CDs, DVDs, or crayons; then help them to recognise the number on the keyboard and type it.

2. Number Paste *see page 65*

List numbers in a row at the top of the page. Create a table, as shown on the next page, with pictures of different numbers of things on one side and blank on the other. Ask your child how many things there are in each row; then either type the number or copy and paste the correct number in the blank space next to the matching picture.

1	2	3	4	5

Start with your child just typing the number in the relevant space; as your child gets used to this game together you can try using the copy and paste feature (see page 68) to move the correct number to the correct picture.

3. Shape counting *see page 66*

Draw outlines onscreen of different common shapes with sides: triangle, squares, hexagons and so on. Together you can count the number of sides the shape has and then ask your child to enter the number of sides into or next to the shape, as shown below.

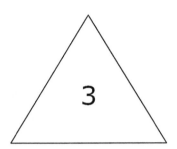

This exercise also builds their recognition of shapes. You can further develop this theme by looking together at shapes of things around the house: the TV or computer screen, the stereo, the clock or picture frame.

Teaching tips

By playing ongoing number games in this way, your toddler is learning in the context of their surroundings and lives which helps to strengthen their new found knowledge.

Digital Art

Artistic Activities

Shapes, colours, pictures, photos and more besides: you and your child have an endless range of art possibilities with the computer.

Art on the PC can be immediate, dynamic and interactive, encouraging your youngster to explore their creativity. As an added bonus they will learn a range of transferable PC skills and programs and find pleasure in completing small projects.

To add interest and variety to working in art, you can introduce some extra hardware. You may have some of these items already. Below is a list of popular devices you and your child could use.

 **Graphic tablet**

 **Digital/video Camera**

 **Webcam**

 **Scanner**

These devices are not particularly expensive and child versions of the cameras are available. For further information, *see page 39.*

The benefits of digital art

A toddler can (with your help) take photos and load them into the computer: then play around with different options: enlarging, different colours, back to front or upside down.

Your child can even add their own creative extras to pictures by colouring in shapes or tracing around a picture with the aid of a graphics tablet. The result of all of their hard work can be printed off for you to display on your fridge!

IT skills

By using extra devices, it will help your child to learn the range of options computers have to quickly change the look of text and pictures.

Motivation

Where projects can be rapidly put together with the help of the computer, your child will be able to start a task and see it through to completion. Just as when you bake cup cakes together, you both feel a sense of achievement at the end, your youngster will feel the same when they have, for example, taken a picture, connected the camera to the computer and printed their photo.

A child's motivation for starting a task will strengthen and grow as they find it leads to a rewarding end result in their work. This important discovery is not just limited to computer technology but will transfer to other areas of life.

Developing self-esteem through trying out a task as well as completing it, helps children feel good about themselves.

Computers today should be a part of everyday life - using different types of equipment will reinforce this

Imagination

Being able to change pictures gives your toddler the opportunity to explore a range of fun possibilities, unrestricted by time, paper or materials. For example, depending on your program, at the click of a button, a grey elephant can be changed to chequered or striped or spotted or back to grey.

Your child can recreate the world they see or change it to what they would like it to be.

Which program?

I wouldn't recommend buying a specific drawing program (like Adobe Photoshop® or CorelDraw®) for your toddler as you will only be using limited features.

Some computer magazines provide a free version of some art programs but there may be a limited amount of time you can use them, usually about 60 days.

Paint®, the program that comes with Microsoft® Windows is sufficient for basic line drawings or using with a graphics tablet.

If you are using an operating system other than Windows, for example, Linux, check with the organisation for the programs that come as standard and for which hardware and software is compatible.

You may also find drawing features in your word processing program.

If you decide to download software from the Internet, make sure it is a safe version and has been checked for viruses with your virus checker or anti-spyware program.

For equipment: if you are using an operating system other than Microsoft® Windows, be sure that any hardware you buy is compatible.

If you have a scanner, it usually comes with software that is suitable for changing the basic format of photographs.

Digital art games

1. Using a word processing program or painting package, you can draw basic shapes for your child to colour in. *See page 67*

If you use the fill button the pictures can be coloured in quickly. Click on the arrow next to the image for a choice of colours.

2. Using either a digital camera or a webcam, you can take pictures of you and your toddler making funny faces together to view on-screen or print out.

3. A picture or photo can be put underneath the film of a graphics tablet; you or your child can then trace over it and colour it in.

4. You and your toddler can take pictures of flowers, animals or things around the house with a digital camera to load onto the PC and then, depending on your program, you can change the colours, flip or rotate the image or add to it with text or colours. You can also do the same with scanned photos. Pictures of familiar people or favourite animals or objects work well.

Refer to your hardware device for instructions.

Multimedia

Music

Children love music - those happy, joyous tunes they (and you) can jump around to. So it would be natural for you to include using the PC as part of this fun.

It has been scientifically proven that music enhances learning by improving the skills needed to understand mathematics and logical thinking.

An easy way to merge technology and music is to use one of your toddler's favourite CDs. Just pop it in the CD or DVD-ROM slot and away you go. If you have Windows media player, your child can watch the various visualisations that move with the beat of the music. These moving images used to keep my son, Mark, entertained for ages.

Music and the Internet

There are many music sites online; downloading music (and videos) now seems to be the preferred choice for a lot people and you are sure to find something that you both like to listen to.

Another activity for you and your youngster is to play various instruments online or sing along to the music for various nursery rhymes.

You should be aware that if you are using a dial-up connection, it may take some time to access what it is that you want. You may also need to download Flash—a type of program that enables moving and dynamic images to be displayed—for some of the objects to work.

Recording

A fun thing you and your toddler can do together is record yourselves singing or talking using a facility available on most PCs. In Windows, you can find this in your Accessories menu. All you need to get started is a microphone.

You and your child then take turns to sing or sing together. Once you have finished recording, you can save your songs on a CD. The result will be a lovely CD for your child to listen to as they go to sleep or when travelling in the car; or even to give to someone as a present.

Video

The great thing about using the PC for video projects is the range of multimedia facilities you have available.

An example of another advantage: to cut out a lot of the arguments from the rest of the family about who watches what on TV, you can find your child's favourite TV programme on the Internet instead. Failing that, if you have a DVD-ROM attached to your computer you can pop in one of their DVDs to entertain them. (Some DVDs often have interactive games as part of the package too—an added bonus.)

Your youngster's own movie

Those of you with video cameras, or even digital cameras with a short video feature (perfect for very young children) you can help your child take short clips to be loaded onto the PC for viewing.

Although throughout this book I have encouraged the use of your own equipment, there are some child's video and digital cameras that are really easy for little fingers to operate.

The robust designs are reassuring to parents in case of any accidents and the features provide many great options for preschool children.

When connecting a device to your PC, including cameras, you may need to install a driver for it to work correctly. Drivers provide information for the PC to help recognise the features of your particular hardware.

A driver comes in the form of a compact disk that is supplied with your device. All instructions for installation come either with the CD or in a user manual. Check them first so your device works correctly.

Computers and special needs

Accessibility for all

Many children with disabilities or special needs can learn to use a computer as confidently as anyone else with the aid of the many devices and software now available on the market.

Likewise thanks to these technical developments parents or carers with disabilities are no longer restricted when it comes to sharing activities with their youngster.

Your operating system may come with accessibility features such as a screen reader or screen magnifier. Newer operating systems have additional accessibility features so it is worth looking through the options to see if they might benefit you.

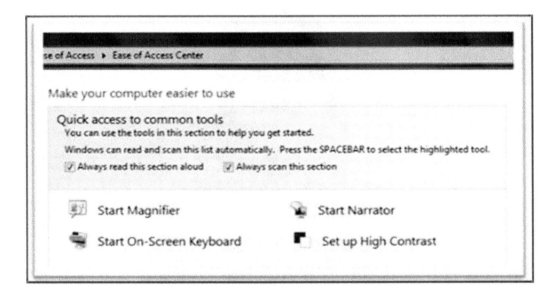

'Accessibility options' or 'Ease of Access Center' can be found in the Control Panel on your PC

Hardware

There are many companies in the marketplace which produce special devices to work with standard PCs.

For example, standard input devices (such as the mouse) have been modified in design to create versions that are larger and those that function ergonomically to enable ease of use for a variety of users.

Also available to you are large keys keyboards and key guards and switches as listed on page 12. The standard switches are table or desk based which can be plugged into the computer via a USB switch interface, but switches can also be wireless or attached to a wheelchair.

For disabilities that restrict mobility in the hands, a head pointer can be used to identify letters on the keyboard.

Touch screen monitors in different sizes enable a user to select information directly on the screen.

Software

There is a huge range of software available for children with disabilities.

As with most software for preschool aged children, there is a fun educational element to the programs for all to enjoy.

'Cause and effect' programs designed to encourage sight and sound recognition, are mostly suitable for children with complex or high support needs, as well as the very young. With their bright flashing colours and loud noises these programs rarely fail to grab a youngster's attention.

Creativity

Using the PC enables your child to enjoy using different aspects and combinations of colour, shapes and sounds in a creative way.

As with any child, the Internet enables youngsters with special needs to view a range of places and countries that would otherwise be difficult to visit in person. There aren't many of us who could observe an Indian elephant in its natural habitat or take in a seaside scene in a single afternoon in the real world.

Your child will have access to some online games, as some now have switch accessibility. Using other available hardware can encourage your preschoolers to instantly produce shapes and pictures as well as to develop auditory and vocal skills.

Further help

For further help with your particular needs, you may find it helpful to contact your local education authority or health and social care department.

For a list of disability related websites *see page 71.*

Summary

There is a role for all of the described products in enhancing youngsters' enjoyment of computers and adding fun and variety to the learning experience. However, there is no substitute for using the real thing: a full-sized, fully functional computer that, with the right help, your preschooler can use easily and confidently.

Young children have the amazing ability to learn, in record time, what some of us may sometimes consider to be a complex piece of equipment. When introduced at such an early age it would become completely natural to youngsters as eating and walking.

Remember that you can help build your child's self-esteem and confidence by:

- Trusting they will make the right choices.
- Allowing them to learn through their mistakes.
- Supporting them when things are not quite right.
- Praising them when they are.
- Asking open questions to encourage language development and problem solving skills

Enjoy watching your youngster's development and achievements on the PC. Most of all have lots of fun together!

Glossary

Administrator – an individual in charge of the technical aspects of the computer systems – usually found in an office setup

Assistive devices – hardware that aids computer use

Browsing – viewing different websites

Caps lock – a button on the keyboard that changes the letters you type to upper case letters

CD-ROM – a disk that stores computer data

Copy and paste – a computer feature of copying text and pictures then placing them in anther part of a document

Dial-up – the use of Internet access through a modem and telephone line

Disk – a storage device containing software or music read by the computer. CDs and DVDs, are all popular types of disks that you can use or save work on

Document – a file

Download – receiving information or graphics from the Internet

Driver – a type of software which helps the computer to recognise different hardware that is attached

Ergonomics – the scientific study of equipment design, for the purpose of improving efficiency, comfort, or safety

Files – a collection of data stored in one unit e.g. a Word processing document

Firewall – an Internet security system that helps to protect your computer system and data

Flash – a software program that enables dynamic images and text to be displayed

Folders – folders on your hard drive store files of a similar nature, e.g., music, pictures or documents

Graphics – images or pictures

Hardware – the physical parts of the computer, e.g., keyboard, mouse

Homepage – the first page that appears when you log onto the Internet

Icons – the images that are shortcuts to functions

Interactive – a two-way system of electronic communications

Internet – a network of computers, allowing millions of people to share information all over the world

Linux – a free operating system

Literacy – the ability to read and write

Logon – a process of gaining access to the computers programs

Modem – a device that enables a computer to transmit data along a telecommunications line.

Multimedia – the integration of multiple forms of media. This includes text, graphics, audio and video

Numeracy – skill with numbers and maths

Operating System – this is the software that communicates with computer hardware

PC – Personal Computer

Pop-up – windows and menus that appear on the screen when surfing the Internet usually information or adverts.

QWERTY – this term is used to describe a standard (Latin alphabet-based) keyboard

Right click – using the right button of the mouse

Scanner – a piece of hardware that copies an image or document onto the computer

Search engine – a program that scans keywords put into a search box

Nicole Taylor

Software – is a general term used to describe a collection of computer programs, procedures and documentation that perform some task on a computer system e.g. MS Office

Spyware – this is software that 'spies' on computer activities getting information about a person without their knowledge

Touch screen – a monitor where you can use touch to select icons and information

USB – Universal Serial Bus, the most common type of computer port (connection) used in today's computers

User licence – comprises the permissions, rights and restrictions imposed on software use

Webcam – a hardware device used for viewing people, places or objects through the computer

Wireless – equipment that can perform without the use of wires

Appendix

Other equipment

Buying products

There is a wealth of computer-related products available, some of which have been discussed already. This section gives you an idea of other devices available both new and second hand that could benefit toddlers and young children and may be worth considering.

The products available to buy for youngsters and young children are designed to have fun learning aims to aid their development such as reading, writing or maths skills.

Games consoles

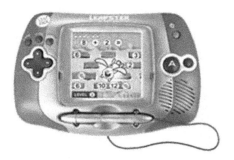

Consoles such as Microsoft® Xbox, Sony Playstation® and Nintendo Wii®, are favourites with children of all ages.

They provide hours of entertainment with the variety of games available to use with them. There are two main types of console – the larger type that you attach to the television and mobile handheld version.

Many toy manufacturers make a handheld version specifically for preschool children. The different games for handheld consoles come in the form of interchangeable cartridges that you place in a slot on the console and are easy for your child to handle.

They can come in different colours and have buttons and controls that are easy to see and use.

For the larger games consoles, such as PlayStation®, some of the games that can be played on the systems are suitable for children from three years onwards.

There are a growing number of interactive consoles and TV games systems that involve players moving parts of the body or their whole body which helps to develop a child's coordination.

TV learning systems

These are consoles that can be attached to the television or – in some cases to a desktop computer. The games have learning goals specific to pre-school children.

The games, that you buy separately, will be in cartridge or compact disc form. Many use popular characters from children's TV to guide youngsters through their learning adventures.

These systems are suitable for ages three to seven years and as with the hand-held consoles; they come in bright colours with large control features.

Interactive books

The activities in these books are suitable for children aged six months to eight years. The devices also use cartridges and also include an interactive book that offer a range of activities. They have a pen attached which is used to select answers, games or text.

Child Laptops

There are lots of colourful, child-friendly laptops made for pre-school children that can be a great intro to computer technology. Preloaded activities introduce various learning elements that aid a child's learning development.

However, you are not able to use standard CDs or DVDs with a child version laptop, connect to the Internet, or add additional hardware devices.

Second desktop computer

With the development of new games for the latest PCs and the rapid progress of change on the Internet, it may be necessary for you to upgrade the computer in order to take advantage of the innovations.

Upgrading usually consists of replacing the hard drive and memory. If you are a novice in upgrading equipment, get product and upgrading advice from someone who is experienced in that field.

You can also use local classifieds for people who want to sell their old computers.

Buying software

There is a huge software market for children's PC games and activities. Many software companies cater for young children from one year old onwards.

PC-ROM games can be reasonably priced and use well known characters for fun and learning activities.

Once you purchase the PC-ROM game there are no other costs which is beneficial if you do not have access to the Internet or use a pay-per-view Internet service with a dial-up modem.

Products Comparisons

Most of the devices have structured learning aims, with instant feedback and also help to develop hand-eye coordination. Below is a summary of advantages and disadvantages between the products discussed earlier in this chapter.

	Advantages	Disadvantages
Games consoles	Can be used by the whole family	Few games with learning goals Can be difficult for very young children to use on their own
Handheld consoles	Mobile Robust	The players neck is in a bent position Each cartridge is purchased individually
TV learning systems	Large features	May be difficult to use if there is one TV in the house
Interactive books	Positive introduction to reading	The books are purchased separately
Additional Software	Access to games if there is no Internet connection Reasonably priced	If you have an older computer some newer games may not work
Child laptops	A variety of pre-loaded activities	Small screen size, usually in black and white Need added attention to posture and desk height due to the size of the equipment
Second PC	Able to use programs that will develop as they grow Able to add extra hard-ware and assistive devices	Additional space Second user licences may be needed for software

How to...

These instructions are for Windows Vista®. For Windows Xp® please refer to the website.

Creating a copy of your work

1. Click on the Start button

2. Click 'All Programs'

3. Click 'Accessories'

4. Click 'System Tools'

5. Click 'Backup status and configuration'

6. Click 'Backup now'

7. Follow the on screen directions

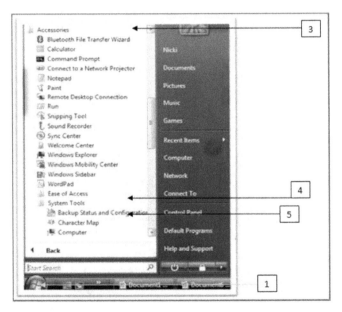

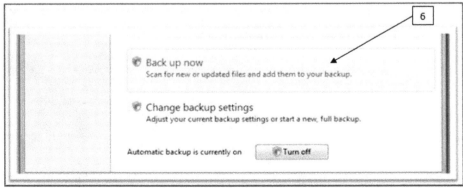

Passwording your files

1. Click on the Office button

2. Click Prepare and then Encrypt document

3. Enter password

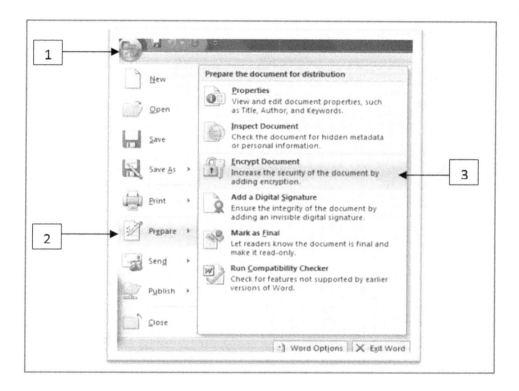

Setting up a separate user profile

1. Click on the 'Start' button

2. Click on 'Control Panel'

3. Click 'Add or remove user accounts'

4. Click on 'Create a new account'

5. Follow onscreen instructions

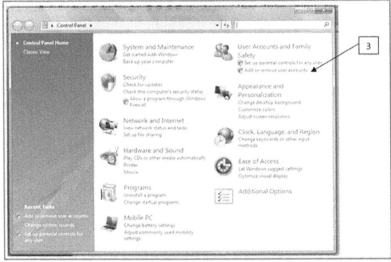

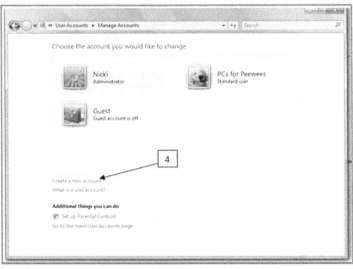

Changing the homepage

1. Click on the tools button on the Internet Explorer menu bar

2. Click on 'Settings' and then Options

3. On the General tab, type in the Web address for your new homepage

4. Click OK

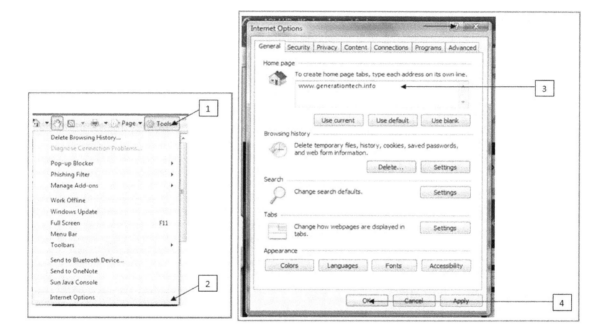

Formatting text

Highlighting text

1. Click at the beginning of the text you want to highlight

2. Keeping the left mouse button pressed down, move the mouse across the text

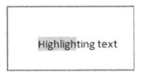

To change the text size

1. Highlight the text

2 Click on the arrow next to the size options

3. Click on the size you want

To change the text colour

1. Highlight the text

2. Click on the arrow next to the colour button

3. Click on the colour you want

Nicole Taylor

To align the text

1. Highlight the text

2. Click on the Align Right button that you require

Left align   Centre align   Right align

Creating a table

1. Click on the Insert tab on the Menu Bar

2. Click 'Table', a grid appears

3. Move the cursor over the grid to get the amount of rows and columns you need

4. Once you have the amount you need in the grid click the left mouse button

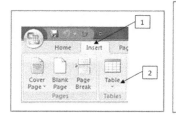

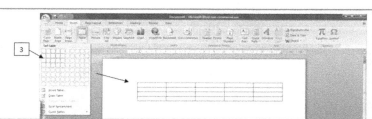

Adding shapes

1. Click on the Insert tab on the menu bar then click on the Shapes button.

2. A list of shapes appears and you can then click on the shape that you want

3. The cursor changes to a cross shape.

4. Click and drag the cursor diagonally on the page to the size you want

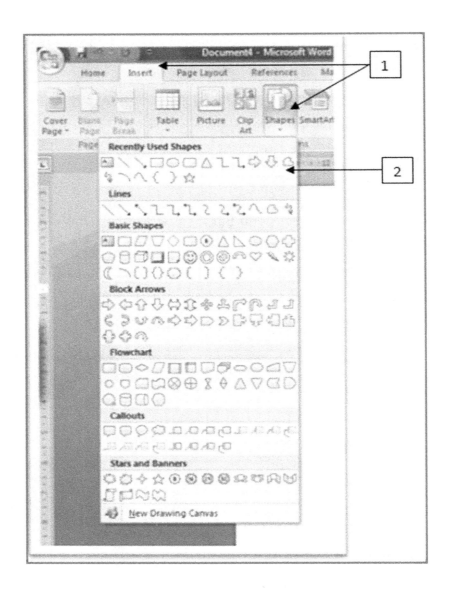

Nicole Taylor

To add text to a shape

1. Click on the shape with the right mouse button

2. From the shortcut menu, click on 'Add Text'

3. Type the text you want and format text as required

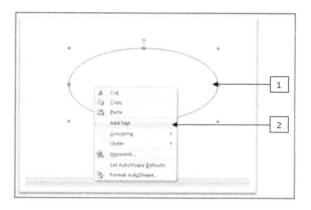

To add colour to a shape

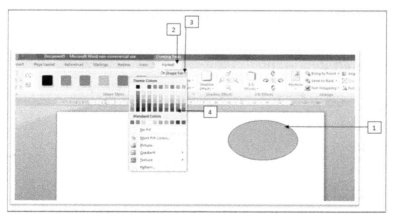

1. Click on the shape with the left mouse button

2. Click on the 'Format' Menu

3. Move the mouse to the arrow next to the Fill button

4. Select your colour

Copy and Paste

1. Highlight the picture or text you want to copy

2. Click on the Copy button

3. Click where you want to paste the picture or text

4. Click the Paste button

Recording sound using Windows

1. Click on the Start button

2. Click 'All Programs' and then on 'Accessories'

3. Click on Sound Recorder

4. Plug in your microphone

5. Click on the 'Start Recording' button

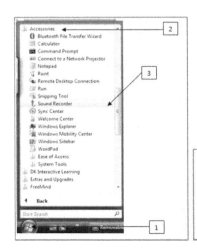

Nicole Taylor

Useful Websites

Activity based websites

As well as your child's favourite TV network channel website, the sites listed below have some fun features for youngsters.

Music Sites

www.niehs.nih.gov/kids/musicchild.htm

www.bussongs.com/

www.mamalisa.com/world/

www.geocities.com/EnchantedForest/Cottage/3192

www.jazzles.com/html/letters.html

www.geocities.com/Athens/Delphi/1794/childrensspanish.html

Activity Sites

www.getreadyforschool.com/links/kidsfun.htm

www.teachersandfamilies.com/open/ps-themes.html

www.lil-fingers.com/links/index.html

http://first-school.ws/

http://lilduckduck.com/toddler-websites-games-activities-and-more/165

Animal Sites

www.seaworld.org/animal-info/sound-library/index.htm

www.davisfarmland.com/fun/funsound.htm

Products and equipment

There is a range of suitable stores that supply hardware, assistive devices and software for preschool age children. Below is a brief list of online stores that deliver in the UK and US; and some delivering worldwide.

www.onestopeducation.co.uk

www.abilitynet.co.uk

www.inclusive.co.uk

www.techready.co.uk

www.curriculumonline.gov.uk

www.onestopshop.co.uk

www.amazon.co.uk

www.tesco.com

www.pcworld.co.uk

www.comet.co.uk

www.woolworths.co.uk

www.shop.avanquest.com

www.amazon.com

www.smartkidssoftware.com

www.kidsclick.com

www.alleducationalsoftware.com

www.bestbuy.com

www.target.com

www.walmart.com

www.learning-apodixis.com/

Nicole Taylor

Disabilities websites

http://www.abilityhub.com/

http://www.apple.com/accessibility/

www.abilitynet.org.uk/

http://microsoft.com/enable/

http://www.head-start.lane.or.us/education/special-needs/computers-children-disabilities.html

http://www.aidis.org/

http://www.learning-apodixis.com/

http://www.thearc.org/

http://www.acd.org.au/information/links.htm

Website addresses correct at time of writing (Jan 2008). We are not endorsing any site and take no responsibility over the content or service for any of the above sites.

Index

About the author

Nicole Taylor has been teaching computer skills to adults, people with disabilities and families for over eight years.

She co-wrote ICT for people with special needs and currently manages a computer project for people with disabilities.

Further information on ICT for toddlers can be found on the website **www.generationtech.info**

www.ingramcontent.com/pod-product-compliance
Lightning Source LLC
Chambersburg PA
CBHW060458060326
40689CB00020B/4579